NATIONAL GEOGRAPHIC

What Makes a Tiger Hard to See?

Louis Capra

Some animals have coverings that make them hard to see. Their coverings blend in with their surroundings.

This tiger lives in
the grasslands.

**What makes the tiger
hard to see?**

3

The stripes on a tiger's fur help it blend in.
It is hard to see a tiger in the long grass.

This frog lives in a pond.

What makes the frog
hard to see?

The frog's green skin helps it blend in.
It is hard to see a frog on a lily pad.

This snowshoe hare lives on a snowy mountain.

What makes the snowshoe hare hard to see?

The snowshoe hare's white fur helps it blend in.
It is hard to see a snowshoe hare in the snow.

This leopard lives in a forest.

What makes the leopard hard to see?

The spots on the leopard's fur help it blend in.

It is hard to see a leopard in the trees.

This sea dragon lives in the ocean.

What makes the sea dragon hard to see?

The shape of a sea dragon's body helps it blend in.
It is hard to see a sea dragon in the seaweed.

This gecko lives in the desert.

What makes the gecko hard to see?

The gecko's sandy-colored skin helps it blend in.
It is hard to see a gecko in the desert sand.

14

This owl lives in a tree.

What makes the owl
hard to see?

The owl's speckled feathers help it blend in.
It is hard to see an owl in a tree.